Geo

Assuuiauuii

Guide No. 65

Edited by J. T. Greensmith

THE ORIGINS OF
STRATIGRAPHY
1719 – 1801

An Historical Guidebook to the Early Days of
Stratigraphical Geology near Bath, Somerset,

as seen in the works of
John Strachey and William Smith
by
John Fuller

THE ORIGINS OF STRATIGRAPHY 1719-1801

AN HISTORICAL GUIDEBOOK TO THE EARLY DAYS OF STRATIGRAPHICAL
GEOLOGY NEAR BATH, SOMERSET
AS SEEN IN THE WORKS OF JOHN STRACHEY AND WILLIAM SMITH

JOHN FULLER

CONTENTS

PREFACE

The purpose of history is to inform the present

This Guide begins with a brief introduction to the first geological work done in England, and goes on to tell the story of events in Somerset associated with the names of two famously gifted pioneers – John Strachey (1671-1743) and William Smith (1769-1839). Most of the Guide's content is focused on an itinerary of places to visit in and near Bath, where these two innovators transformed colliers' lore and cabinet curiosities into scientific stratigraphy.

This itinerary can be completed in one full day, though using a car in the congested city of Bath can be difficult. Tour sites in the city are best approached on foot. There is, at the time of writing, a Park-and-Ride system that runs frequently and efficiently from several places on the city margin. Street names, car parks, and National Grid lines in the city are marked on a 1:10,000-scale Bath City Map published by the Ordnance Survey. In rural areas the most useful map is Sheet 172 of the 1:50,000 Ordnance Survey series. At some rural sites narrow lanes may hinder access by vehicles larger than a minibus.

As well as the more obvious maps needed to find one's way, numerous local pamphlets can be found with the assistance of the Bath Tourism and Conference Bureau. For example, two usefully compact items are the Bath Scientific Heritage Trail and Tucking Mill Trail Guide.

The author warmly acknowledges permission by the American Association of Petroleum Geologists and the British Geological Survey to reproduce copyright material, and thanks the Curator of Geological Collections, University Museum, Oxford, and the Somerset County Archivist, for permitting access to archived material. National Grid coordinates are used with kind permission of the Ordnance Survey. In addition, my personal thanks go to Professor D. T. Donovan for substantial advice.

LIST OF FIGURES

Photographs and illustrations are by the author, unless otherwise acknowledged.

INTRODUCTION

Geology of the Strata in England Before 1719

Knowledge of stratified rocks in England sprang directly from the industrial experience of artisan workmen employed as miners, colliers, quarrymen, well-borers, wallers, stonemasons, and salters. From the earliest days to the beginning of the nineteenth century three mineral commodities – coal, iron-ore, and building-stone – embraced virtually all practical knowledge of stratified rocks. This came about because experience of mining coal, quarrying stone, and digging ore had taught working men hard facts about the nature of strata, facts such as their variations of quality, substance, thickness and structural attitude. Miners underground were acutely aware of abrupt and unforeseen dislocations and terminations of strata, cutting off working seams, and sometimes lives. Searching for, and producing any mineral commodity required a particular set of skills that could be learned only by practice, not least the skill to judge between a mineral's economic worth and the hazards of getting it.

Observations on the economy of coal-working and salt-extraction were being gathered in England as long ago as the 1540s, when King Henry VIII commissioned John Leland to 'peruse the secrets of antiquity' and to compile a country-wide survey that would embrace everything from monastic libraries to mineral deposits. Leland journeyed for several years through most of England and Wales, noting among the thousands of facts recorded in his collected *Itinerary* the presence or absence of stone-quarrying, salt-working, and coal-pits. He even commented on the likely continuation of a coal-stratum beneath Durham Cathedral.

All geological information in Leland's great work was obtained either directly from workmen or from his own observation, establishing him as the first major figure in England to bridge the gap between compilers of book-learning and artisans of industry. Through the 17th and 18th centuries, authors of geological works were commonly unaware of artisan experience, chiefly because artisans kept their secrets to themselves, and did not reveal to strangers knowledge that was the source and support of their livelihood. Even in modern times this disjunction persists, separating academic scholars from the operating technicians of industry.

Minerals of economic worth were generally worked underground, so somewhat unexpectedly the geology of rocks at surface outcrop did not become important in scientific thinking until the regularity of strata and their ordered arrangement underground had been already realized. Through the 1600s, records of strata, along with their various properties and characteristics, were commonly made in the form of lists or tables, mostly constructed from the results of subsurface operations (Figure 1).

Such examples demonstrate that miners, well-borers, shaft-sinkers and other artisans possessed practical experience and familiarity with the nature of stratified rocks, yet it was only by the rare appearance of an individual capable of bridging the gap between industrial practice and book learning, that is to say someone capable of speaking and understanding both languages, could geological knowledge pass out of coal-pits and industrial workings, and be spread among scientists and scholars.

1

At Sutton and Faringdon in Somerſetſhire, from my own Obſervation, the Dip is S. E.

	feet.
Yellowiſh Earth	2
Beds of Lyas	10
Yellowiſh Loom	6
Blue Clay	3
Lighter Blue Loom	3
Deep blue Malm ſoft and ſoapy.	3
Marcheſite	6
Deep blue Marl	4
RedEarth &Malm	60
Red Fireſtone	2
Grey Millſtone	2 or 3
Coal Clives	35
Coal the Stinking Vein 1 *f.* 8	20
Clives and Dung	42 *f.*
Cathead Vein	2 *f.* 6
Dung and Clives	42 *f.*
Three Coal Vein	3 *f.*
Hard Cliff with Cokles and Fern Branches - *f.*	48
Peau Vein with Peacocks Eyes *f.*	2
Cliff	33 *f.*
Smiths Coal	3 *f.*
Cliff	36 *f.*
Shelly Vein	2 *f.* 6
Cliff	36 *f.*
Ten-Inch Vein	10 *f.*

***Figure 1** (left)*

A stratigraphic column or table, one of fourteen such examples collected and published in 1727 by John Strachey, F.R.S. The thicknesses of these beds came from a Somerset coal-pit, and represent the first stage of making a stratigraphic cross-section of underground strata. The Marchesite, a bed of laminated clay 'much impregnated with iron-pyrites' was six inches thick, not six feet. The Stinking Vein was 20 inches thick, not 20 feet, and the Ten-inch Vein was ten inches thick, not ten feet.

Two such accomplished and observant individuals, John Strachey (1671-1743) and William Smith (1769-1839) are the principal subjects of this Guidebook. Quite remarkably, nearly every event in their segment of geological history, from John Strachey's invention in 1719 of stratigraphic cross-sections, to William Smith's realisation in 1796 that each stratum could acquire a separately distinctive identity from the fossils found in it, took place in a small area of northeastern Somerset between Bath and Mendip, mainly in the parishes of Chew Magna, Stowey, High Littleton and Dunkerton. Yet it is now evident that far more than geographical proximity entwines the names of John Strachey and William Smith in this modest little tale of detective geology.

John Strachey (1671-1743)

The story of John Strachey, William Smith, and the origin of English stratigraphy begins with a lease drawn up in April 1719, entitling William Jones of Stowey to 'Search for open dig or Sink any pitt or pitts for Coal' on certain lands belonging to John Strachey of Sutton Court (Figure 2) in the parish of Chew Magna, *juxta* Stowey. The two men were in fact brothers-in-law, residing within half a mile of one another. Whether William Jones ever sank a shaft or coal-pit on his Sutton lease is not known, but we do know that Strachey had made a study of nearby coal-works at Bishop Sutton, about half a mile southwest of Sutton Court, and at Stanton Drew, about a mile to the north. He had also learned from colliers that the same group of coals found at Sutton was also being worked in pits toward Farrington Gurney, about four miles southeast of Sutton Court. Strachey's lands lay between the productive areas, and to demonstrate their potential value (supposedly for his brother-in-law) he made a diagram in the form of a cross-section showing the probable subterranean arrangement of the coals, their thicknesses, and depths (Figure 3).

Strachey wrote a letter explaining the geology of the local coal industry and the nature of the strata to his friend Robert Welsted, M.D., who was a Fellow of the Royal Society. The letter set down methods used by Somerset colliers for measuring strike orientations, angles of dip and thicknesses of the various strata in the mines; and Strachey made a point of saying that all the subterranean details were given to him by the colliers. Welsted communicated this letter to the Society at its meeting on May 7th, 1719, and arrangements were made for its publication, along with the explanatory cross-section. Strachey was then forty-eight years of age, squire, antiquarian, and well known in the county. In November the Royal Society elected him to Fellowship.

For Strachey's earlier life and his antiquarian pursuits, the archive is patchy. He was at heart a collector of facts, industriously dedicated to their every detail, yet he was less able than he might have been at gathering them into a connected narrative. Neverthless, when Strachey hands you a geological observation, such as 'coal strata in the pit at Bishop Sutton dip at 22 inches in a fathom' you know it to be trustworthy, a fact that he had learned from the colliers, and could be measured on his section (Figure 3).

Variants of Strachey's diagram were produced in 1721, 1725, 1727 and 1734, the last three extending the original four-mile length of section to more than twenty miles, spanning a tract from the Chalk hills of Wiltshire to high ground above Wrington, near Bristol. Accompanying them were strike-sections crossing at right-angles from the Marlborough Downs to Mendip. In a second paper for the Royal Society published in 1725, and also in a separately issued booklet (1727), Strachey emphasised his conception of the *Strata* as a body or group of layered earths and minerals extending from the coast of Wessex north-eastward to Yorkshire and the coast of Northumberland. This he knew from his own observations, having in 1721 visited the northern counties on his way to Scotland. The *Strata* as he understood them were potentially of global extent.

'All these different *Strata*, as found in any of those Places I have observed myself, or met with from others, I have at one View represented in a globular Projection of the terraqueous Globe.'

3

Figure 2. Sutton Court, the south aspect from Collinson's Somerset, 1791. Photograph by courtesy of the Society of Antiquaries of London.

4

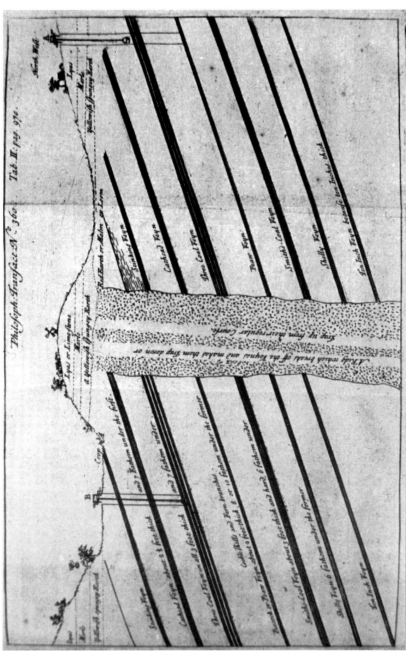

Figure 3. John Strachey's 'Section of a Coal-Country,' 1719. Most or the subsurface geology illustrated could not have been observed at the surface, and was made by correlating strata underground from coal-pit to coal-pit. This diagram was a template for later cross-sections, and afterwards exerted unmistakable influence on William Smith's sectional drawings. An account of Strachey's construction of this subsurface section, and others like it, can be found in Archives of Natural History, v.19, p.69-90, 1992.

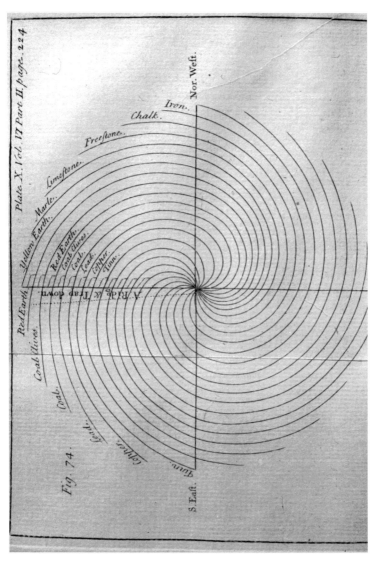

Figure 4. Strachey's global view or 'globular projection' of the Strata, 1725. The stratigraphic sequence of twelve named units rotates from east to west, going down in sequence from Wealden iron to Chalk, Cotswold Freestone, then Lias limestone, Marle, and Yellow Earth, thence through Red Earth to Coal Clives to Coal, and further to the Lead-bearing Limestone of Mendip and Broadwell Down, thence more westerly to Cornish Tin and Copper. At that level the series replicates. 'Clives' means 'Cleaves' or fissile rocks.

Strachey's *Strata*, so defined, consisted of several discrete entities in stratigraphic succession. At the top, *Chalk* (Upper Cretaceous), followed downward by *Freestone* (Upper & Middle Jurassic), *Lias and Marl* (Lower Jurassic), *Red Earth* (Triassic), *Clives and Coal* (Upper Carboniferous), and *Limestone with Lead* (Lower Carboniferous). This sequence he expanded to twelve units or parts by the addition of other earths, ochres, and metals, so that the *Strata* came to be seen as a duodecimally-ordered fabric covering the whole earth or 'terraqueous globe'. He visualised the rotating earth as consisting of twenty-four individual layers, twelve of which were exposed to the passing day at a rate of one per hour, and a further twelve duplicating exactly the same sequence at night (Figure 4).

One might unthinkingly dismiss all this as curious whimsy, though its author was in fact addressing a serious philosophical topic that in 1725 his Royal Society audience would have well appreciated, namely an 'argument from design'. His idea could certainly be understood as a testimony that *Design* revealed *Order*; and that the order so revealed among the strata was likely to be universal, a high and ancient order manifested by Providence at the beginning of the world. Both themes, the rotating strata and the natural order, were to be taken up later by William Smith.

'Stonehenge Stukeley' and the Easterly Dip

One day in the summer of 1723, William Stukeley (1687-1765) accompanied John Strachey on a visit to the ancient stone circles of Stanton Drew, near Sutton Court. Both men were absorbed in antiquarian studies, which in those days could include anything 'old', even fossils. In fact, Strachey showed Stukeley some fern-leaf impressions on slabs of shale brought from a local coal mine, and their conversation turned to questions concerning the nature of strata, in particular the general easterly dip of coal strata underground. Strachey said that the miners denied any dip among strata above ground, though Stukeley already had seen easterly dip at the surface, and said so in his great volume *Itinerarium Curiosum*, published during the following year. He mentioned Strachey and the ferns, and dwelt at length on the subject of easterly dip:

> 'I see no difficulty to attribute the reason of it to the rotation of the globe ... Tis a property of matter that when whirl' d round upon an *axis*, it endeavours to fly from the *axis*, as we see in the motion of a wheel... Now at the time when the body of the earth was in a mixt state between solid and fluid, before its present form of land and sea was perfectly determined, the almighty Artist gave it its great diurnal motion. By this means the elevated parts or mountainous tracts, as they consolidated whilst yet soft and yielding, flew somewhat westward and spread forth a long declivity to the east; the same is to be said of the plains, their natural descent trending that way, and as I doubt not, of the superfice of the earth below the ocean….The truth of this observation I have seen universally confirm'd in all my travels.'

This gripped Strachey's imagination, and in 1725, when he read his second paper to the Royal Society, he made a global representation of his stratigraphic ideas, using Stukeley's explanation for eastward-sloping landscapes. Evidently, at this period in the 18th century not much distinction was being made either by Stukeley or Strachey between the slope of a plane or flat land-surface and the slope of a stratum.

'In all places within my knowledge', wrote Strachey, 'the observation of Dr. Stukely has held good, that the precipices of all hills are to the westward, whereas the ascent to the east is more gradual.'

Strachey's diagram (Figure 4) has earned more than its share of ridicule. John Phillips, in his biography of William Smith, went out of his way to say that it was a 'childish hypothesis'. Yet its logic was sound, and its pedigree immaculate. Seventeenth-century schooling at any level offered but one area of common ground where discussion of Earth's history could take place, namely the Biblical narratives. For example, verses 9-13 of the first chapter in the book of Genesis gave an account of events on the third day of Creation, from which we can learn how our forebears, geological or otherwise, were taught that the origin of the strata was virtually an instantaneous event, the whole appearing as one, not by parts. Continuing then to the fourth day of Creation, verses 14-19 of the same narrative made clear to everyone that the rotative motion of the globe, from east to west, began after the strata had been formed, and for that reason, while still unconsolidated, the strata came to recline in stacked arrays, scarps to the west and long surfaces of gentle dip eastward. All this is now so obvious that it hardly bears explanation; and it will cause no amazement to find that William Smith was much impressed by it, noting that the strata had bent or warped into their easterly-dipping attitude at the commencement of terrestrial rotation, while they were still plastic:

'And the motion of the earth, which probably commenced while these strata were in a soft state or of a pulpy consistence, would naturally place them in an inclined curvilineal position.'

Smith also adopted Strachey's picture of cyclic strata, counting the day's twenty-four hour rotation by an equal number of beds:

'Thursday Sep 6th 1798
To make this more inteligable we will suppose a spectator (divested of attraction and stationed at rest to observe the strata of the circumference as they pass by him while the earth turns round) to begin at one of the most remarkable of those beds that when he comes to the same point again he may know that he has noticed them all and completed an imaginary survey which may do well to illustrate our theory'

Actually, all three of them in turn, Stukeley, Strachey and Smith, were repeating an old collier's adage that could be found in John Ray's *Three Physico-Theological Discourses* of 1713, saying that 'Coals lie one way, and do always dip towards the East' and that were it not for the water 'they might pursue the Bed of Coals to the very Center of the Earth'. It was one of the features of Strachey's somewhat bewildering conception of Earth's structure (Figure 4), that all strata shelved eastward down to the centre.

John Strachey continued his geological pursuits after publishing the 1727 booklet,

8

adding to it many more handwritten pages. He compiled a description of the strata of England and parts of Wales from his own observations made on journeys that took him from the southern counties through the Midlands and northeast to Northumberland and Scotland. But it was not published for he was by then trapped in financial and family shortcomings. His heir, Hodges Strachey, reputed to be an extravagant fellow, had the management of the Sutton Court estate. Strachey's ever-patient wife Elizabeth died at Edinburgh in 1722, while her husband was occupied with his work in Scotland. He himself lived until 1743, and died at Greenwich.

With his passing, scientific and geological interest in the neighbourhood of Chew Magna and Stowey seems to have lapsed, at least until 1783, when a group of eight partners took up leases to open a coal work on property at High Littleton belonging to Mary Jones of Stowey, Strachey's niece. This colliery was at Mearns (Figure 5) at ST 653588, about five hundred yards north of the manor house called Rugbourne, which also belonged to her. Mary Jones died in 1791, and her estate went to a cousin in Wiltshire, though not before probate of her will, for which a survey and valuation were needed. In October of that year a young man from Gloucestershire arrived to make the survey, by name William Smith.

William Smith (1769-1839)

All that is known of William Smith's early life, or virtually all, was collected in a biography published in 1844 by his nephew, John Phillips. Smith was born on March 23, 1769, into the family of an Oxfordshire blacksmith. His schooling was rudimentary. He was an orphan at eight, and was sent to work on an uncle's farm. In such poor circumstances, a rural orphan boy picking stones off the frozen fields in winter might not have been heard of again; but by singular good fortune, young Smith's intelligence and industry were noticed by a sharp-eyed land surveyor, Edward Webb, who took him in as an assistant. Webb conducted his surveying business from Stow-on-the-Wold, a small market town high in the Cotswold Hills of Gloucestershire. Agricultural surveying was at that time a fast-expanding activity, a response to the trend toward enclosing land in which root-crops could be grown, thus making possible the over wintering of livestock, and so increasing landowners' profits. Enclosure of agricultural land accelerated as manufacturing industries boomed and urban populations grew. Impossibly bad roads in areas where heavy industry was developing encouraged the construction of new canals for bulk carriage inland (Figure 6). One such project, the Somersetshire Coal Canal, became a key feature of Smith's early career.

At Stow-on-the-Wold, Smith lived with the Webb family for nearly five years, training himself to the disciplines of land surveying, assisting with surveys of lands scheduled for enclosure, making agricultural valuations, and managing improvements to farmland drainage. He said later that he grew into the habit of observing the ground under his feet wherever his work for Mr. Webb took him. Away from the improved turnpikes, roadways in the country commonly revealed bare rock. Also, of course, Smith's work as a surveyor of agricultural land would always have focused his attention on local soil character, methods of wetland drainage, and the nature of the bedrocks.

When in 1791 the recently-widowed Lady Elizabeth Jones of Ramsbury, Wiltshire, found

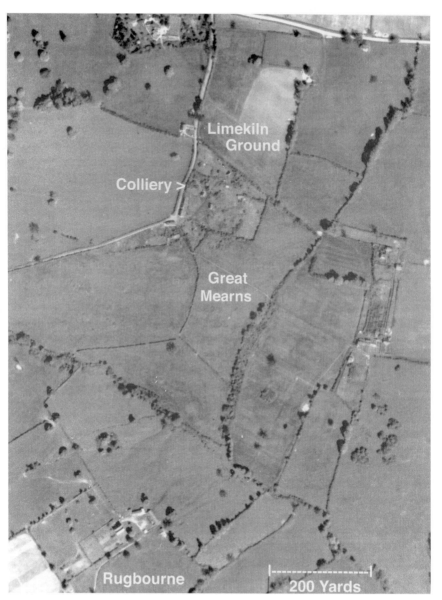

Figure 5. Aerial photograph of the site of Mearns Colliery and Rugbourne Farm. Between Rugbourne and Mearns signs of shale tips and old coal workings at the surface were still visible when this 1947 photograph was made. North is at the top of the Figure.

10

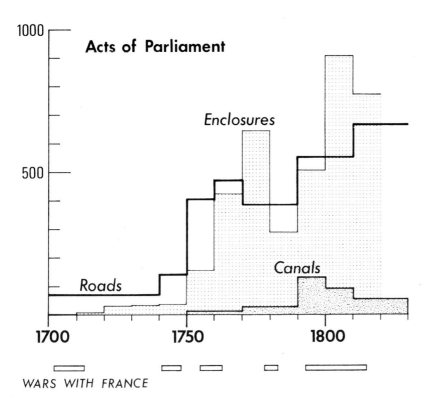

1000 — Acts of Parliament

Enclosures

500

Canals

Roads

1700   1750   1800

WARS WITH FRANCE

Figure 6. Comparative frequencies of Acts of Parliament relating to enclosures of land and construction of roads and canals, showing also periods of warfare between Britain and France. Enclosures are shown in decades, 1700-1820; roads and canals are shown as averages for decades in 10-, 20-, or 40-year periods, 1700-1830. This diagram reveals the great surge of activity called the Industrial Revolution. Source: Bulletin of the American Association of Petroleum Geologists, 1969, v.53, p.2256 - 73.

herself wanting a surveyor to make a probate valuation of property she had inherited from a deceased cousin in Somerset, Mary Jones of Stowey, she turned to Edward Webb of Stow, who sent Smith to make the survey. For the future course of geology, those dry facts were to become highly significant because Lady Jones's deceased cousin was the last surviving neice of John Strachey, the same John Strachey who in 1719 had published a description of geology in the Stowey area, and had drawn a cross-section to illustrate the coal-lease he gave to Mary Jones's father, showing how the various seams of coal below ground lay in relation to one another and to the overlying strata in the hills above. Strachey's lands and those of the Jones family adjoined in such a way that his original cross-section represented parts of both.

11

Transcript of an Original Document by William Smith
Illustrating a Plan of Mearns Coalwork
Surveyed in 1791-92

Original Sketch and observations of my first subterranean Survey
of Mearns Colliery in the Parish of High Littleton

1 The pitt, 100 Yards deep where the Coal is landed by a Machine turned by a Horse which consists of a large upright Axle (and braces) --- feet high on the upper part of which is fixed a Drum wheel --- feet Diam: and --- feet thick at the Circumference having a rim or Board on its upper and lower edges projecting out, and another round the middle which divides it in two part round which coils two Ropes running over two Rollers and two little Wheels --- feet Diam: just over the pitt to the ends of these two Ropes the Baskets (call'd Bushells) are hook'd on and as the empty one goes down on one Rope the full one comes up on the other to the top when the full one is unhook'd at the Top and the empty one at the Bottom. And the Horse turns and drives the Machine the contrary way which lets down the empty one and draws up the full one as before and so on alternately ---

2 A Standing --- is a place by the side of the bottom of the Pitt at the top of the Gugg abt. 8 or 10 feet high where is fixed a Windlass (turn'd by Men) with a large Balance wheel on it round the Axle of which coils two Ropes to the ends of which are hook'd two 3 Bushell Carts (on four low Wheels) which running up and down the Guggs the empty one going down and the full one coming up at the same time which is pitch'd down in the standing and loaded into the Bushell Baskets that come down the Pitt ---

[Smith's sketch of Mearns' Colliery was inserted here.]

3 A Gugg --- is a common Road about 4 feet high and --- wide and 55 yards long --- Pitches abt.9 Inches in a Yard in the Bottom lies Timber framed together down which are two Roads on four Ruttsmade for the Wheels of the Carts to run in so as to pass one by the other going up an down.

4 A Twinway --- a common Road from the Bottom of the first Gugg to the Standing at the top of the Second about 4 feet high --- feet wide and 40 yards long and nearly on the level. The 3 Bushel Carts that are wound up the Second Gugg are drawn along here to the bottom of the first by a Man down on his hands and feet, bare, with a Cord round his Waist, to which is fastened a Chain that comes between his legs and hooks to the forepart of the Cart.

5 a Standing --- the same as 2--

6 a Gugg pitches 1 foot in a Yard abt. 40 Yards long in other respects like 3 ---

7 a Standing the same as 2---

8 a Gugg the same as 3---

9 a Standing the same as 2---

10 a Gugg the same as 3, abt. half way down on the right hand side is a new pitt sunk down into the little Vein ---

11 New pitt sunk into the little Vein 9 Yards deep

12 A pitt abt. 11 Yards deep where the Coal is drawn up from the Little Vein by a Windlass in Baskets and there pitcht in a Standing and loaded into the 3 Bushel Carts that come down the Guggs

Figure 7. (left) William Smith's Original Sketch of my first subterranean Survey, transcribed from the original at the University Museum, Oxford. The numbers 1-12 relate to those in Figure 8 (below).

William Smith's initial work on the Jones estate in 1791 and 1792 was the probate survey and valuation of the late Mary Jones's farmlands, tenancies, and buildings, including the colliery at Mearns (ST 652588) near his lodging at Rugbourne Farm. Again, the only account of events attending Smith's arrival at Stowey is to be found in John Phillips's Memoirs of William Smith (1844):

> 'Coal was worked at High Littleton beneath the 'red earth', and I was desired to investigate the collieries and state the particulars to my employer. My subterraneous survey of these coal veins, with sections which I drew of the strata sunk through in the pits, confirmed my notions of some regularity in their formation.' The minute survey which Mr. Smith made of the High Littleton Collieries was continued at intervals through the years 1792 and 1793, and among the papers remaining, which demonstrate a perfect acquaintance with the effect of the faults, on the outcrops and depths of the coal, are an 'Original Sketch and Observations of my first Subterranean Survey of Mearn's Colliery in the parish of High Littleton'.

Smith surveyed Mearns in 1792, and the *Original Sketch and Observations of my first Subterranean Survey*, mentioned in the passage quoted above, is one of two undated though closely related papers in the Smith archive at Oxford. A new transcription of this *Original Sketch* is given here (Figure 7) together with Smith's plan of the colliery (Figure 8). This plan can be correlated with an aerial view showing its position on the ground (Figure 5). A second paper has the title *Small Sketch & Section & acct of Mearns Coalwork*. This is a pen and ink drawing of the mine elevation, with its subterranean inclines. At some time after it had been made, the drawing was entirely brushed over with an obliterating coat of black ink or pigment. One might argue that the black colouration was simply an experiment to show the drawing in the same colour as the coalpit, for Smith certainly favoured self-coloured representation of strata on his later maps and sections. The line-drawing itself under the wash of black pigment, reveals Smith's first known colliery section. On it, stations within the mine are numbered from 1 to 12, exactly corresponding to the plan accompanying his *Original Sketch and Observations* (Figure 8). No geological matter appears in either of these papers, though in the meantime Smith had apparently become aware of Strachey's cross-section, a copy of which came to light in 1938 among Smith's papers surviving at Oxford, marked with words and numbers in Smith's own hand, and noting the throw of subsurface faulting in coal-seams that Strachey had illustrated (Figure 9). By 1793, Smith was thinking of making and colouring his own sections of strata 'as found in the sinking of coal mines'.

For three years, Smith continued to lodge at Rugbourne. He was then twenty-four years of age and well established locally as a land surveyor with some knowledge of coal. By force of character and technical ability he persuaded a committee of mine-owners in the district to employ him in the work of surveying and taking levels for their newly projected canal, by which they planned to move coal from local collieries down to a new long-distance waterway connecting Bristol with London (Figure 10). During 1793, plans and estimates for the coal-canal were drawn up, and in 1794 he was appointed surveyor and resident engineer. Though scant record remains of Smith's coal-canal work during the years

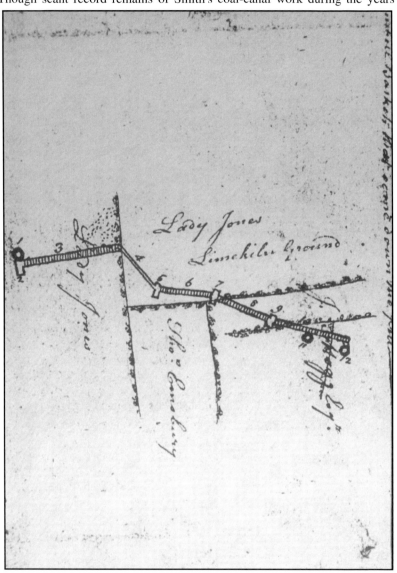

Figure 8. William Smith's plan of Mearns Colliery, part of his Original Sketch of my first subterranean Survey *(Figure 7). Field names can be correlated with an aerial photograph (Figure 5).*

14

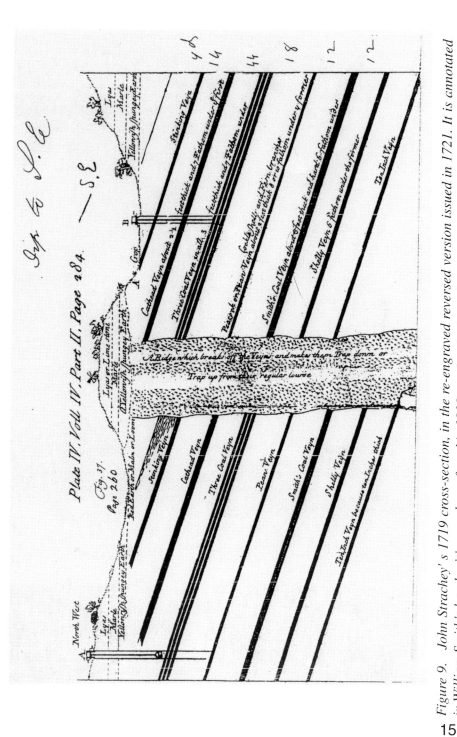

Figure 9. John Strachey's 1719 cross-section, in the re-engraved reversed version issued in 1721. It is annotated in William Smith's handwriting, and was found in 1938, or shortly thereafter, at Oxford among a collection of papers left by Professor John Phillips, Smith's nephew. Of some significance, Smith noted on his cross-section where, 'Page 260,' he could find and read Strachey's original accompanying text.

15

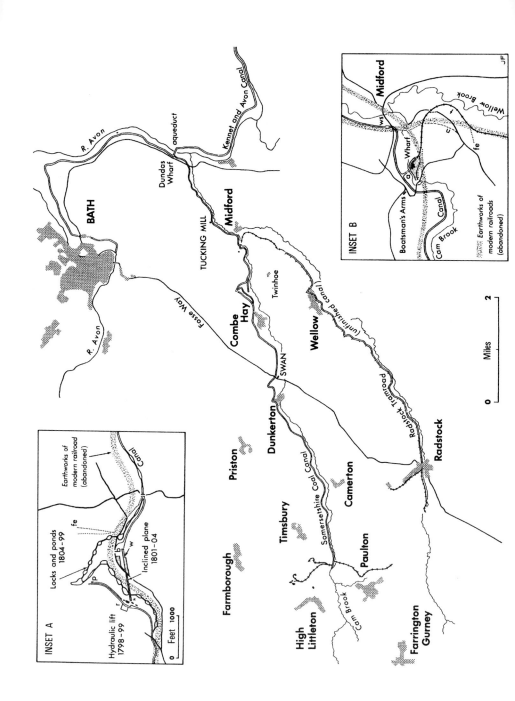

BATH

R. Avon

R. Avon

Dundas Wharf

aqueduct

Kennet and Avon Canal

TUCKING MILL

Fosse Way

Midford

Combe Hay

Twinhoe

SWAN

Wellow

(unfinished canal)

Dunkerton

Priston

Farmborough

Timsbury

Camerton

Paulton

Somersetshire Coal Canal

High Littleton

Cam Brook

Radstock Tramroad

Radstock

Farrington Gurney

0   1   2

Miles

INSET A

Hydraulic lift 1798–99

Locks and ponds 1804–99

Earthworks of modern railroad (abandoned)

Canal

fe

w

b

p

Inclined plane 1801–04

0   Feet   1000

INSET B

Midford

Midford

Wellow Brook

ws

Wharf

a

t

u

fe

Boatsman's Arms

Cam Brook

Canal

Earthworks of modern railroads (abandoned)

JF

16

Figure 10. (left) Reference map of the Somersetshire Coal Canal area, with inset maps showing construction works where upper and lower levels of the Canal met.
Inset A:
Combe Hay, about 1798-1899. A hydrostatic lift for boats utilising the principle of a moving caisson suspended in a vertical water-filled chamber was tried, but it failed and was abandoned in 1799. An inclined plane for trans-shipping coal was substituted, Abbreviations, Inset A: w -wharves at foot of inclined plane; b -basin; r- reservoir.
Inset B:
Midford, about 1802-1871. The Radstock tramroad, built mainly on the towing path of the uncompleted branch of the Canal, descended by an earlier stretch of tram-road from an upper level near Twinhoe to a wharf near Midford, where it connected with a spur canal from the lower level of the main line. The tram-road or 'drammy road' of local memory ceased operation about 1871.
Abbreviations, Inset B (same scale as A): t -tram-road; a- aqueduct; fe -fullers-earth road; n -new road (post Somerset and Dorset railway); ws -boat weighing-station.

1794 to 1799, a few uniquely valuable words happen to have been saved, written by him on a scrap of paper dated January 5, 1796. The words express his astonishment that fossil occurrences in nature – assemblages of fossils as well as specific kinds – were governed by the same systematic order as the strata themselves. Of all the original observations made by Smith, this is the most celebrated and most deeply impressed in geological literature. The principle appears in many forms, but most expressively in Smith's own words:

'D. Swan 1796- Jany 5th (Page 2) *Fossils* have been long studdied as great Curiosities collected with great pains treasured up with great Care and at a great Expence and shown and admired with as much pleasure as a Childs rattle or his Hobby horse is shown and admired by himself and his playfellows – because it is pretty. And this has been done by Thousands who have never paid the least regard to that wonderful order & regularity with which Nature has disposed of these singular productions and assigned to each Class its peculiar Stratum –'

A second manuscript fragment, undated, records substantially the same sentiment, crediting the disposition of fossils to the 'Creator' in place of 'Nature', This note is headed Fossils :

'Many men to gratify mere Curiosity & to no other end have been at infinite pains to collect choice Specimens from the numerous Fossil Tribe without so much as dreaming of that Systematic arrangement to which they are the best of all Indieces – or paying the least attention to that regularity with which the Creator has disposed of these singular productions & assigned to each Class its peculiar Stratum –'

The point of presenting both quotations is that they are mutually supportive, indicating that Smith did mean what he said: that the *Stratum* defined the fossils. This principle so stated was actually the converse of what he, and others after him, actually put into practice. Adding also to this matter of historical accuracy, Smith's use of the word order in 'that wonderful order' which was so apparent to him, was the order of nature - *a high and ancient order, written by the finger of God himself.* It had nothing to do with sequential-order, ranking-order, hierarchy, relative age or geological time. History can be carelessly damaged by reading new meanings into old words.

Smith set down on paper his momentous discovery at the Swan Inn, Dunkerton, only a few yards from the newly excavated bed of the coal canal. The actual date when the observation was made, and the place, can be related exactly to the progress of construction on the canal. Tenders for cutting the canal bed were called in 2-mile sections, starting in June 1795. The *Bath Chronicle* of May 7th, 1795, carried this advertisement:

'The Committee will be ready on the 2nd June to receive proposals to contract for cutting, embanking, puddling, and compleating that part of the canal from Paulton engine to Hopyard, being in length about two miles.'

On July 30th the *Bath Chronicle* similarly advertised for cutting the next section, as far as the Swan Inn, Dunkerton, and in the issue of November 26th advertisements appeared for tenders to cut a further two miles beyond the Swan. There was therefore every reason for Smith to have been at the Swan early in January, 1796, puzzling to himself why the several layers of rock that he had so far excavated seemed to contain different sorts of fossil shells. On the main line of the canal the first length crossed barren Triassic red beds; the second length, which by the end of 1795 had reached the Swan Inn, Dunkerton, was cut mainly through fossiliferous beds of Lower Jurassic (Lias shale and Midford Sand) and Middle Jurassic (Inferior Oolite limestone). Contrasts of rock colouration and fossil-assemblage among the freshly exposed strata, and their slight dip away from the canal level toward the southeast, so impressed Smith that he decided to begin surveying the strata of the surrounding area as well. Using a locally made plan scaled at 1.5 miles to 1 inch as his base map, he laid down colors to show where each stratum emerged at the surface. His base map bore no indication of topography or ground elevation, yet what he achieved was in every way a stratigraphic map. He drew the actual position on the ground where the lower edge of each stratum emerged, colouring it darker to provide some effect of solidity. The delineations as he saw them were not pristine arcs of intercept made by basal planes emerging on a smoothly uniform global surface, but winding and intricately sinuous traces that in his view emerged on a surface made uneven, degraded, and worn by flood-waters of the Biblical Deluge. Isolated pieces of strata that were detached from their main bodies, like islands standing in a flood, Smith called insular knolls; and areas of a stratum scoured through and revealing the stratum next below, as through a window, he called denudations. In June of the same year, 1799, at a house in Bath, Smith supervised the writing out of a *Table of Strata*, dictating particulars of its 23 named and identified component units, their

18

individual thicknesses, their characteristic fossils, and other features, to his close friend Benjamin Richardson. So strongly did Smith believe that his method of delineating strata could be extended to the whole country that by 1801 he had made a small-scale map of England and Wales showing the distribution of the strata. Furthermore, he had composed some six thousand words toward a projected treatise to be entitled *Natural Order of Strata*; but Smith's creative genius was balked by a poverty of schooling, for which all his artisan skills could not compensate. The introductory preface to Smith's *Natural Order of Strata* was published by L.R. Cox in 1942.

A short aside on William Smith's use of the term stratum may not be out of place. He had very likely inherited it from John Strachey's work, and even in the language of the 1790s, it was growing somewhat old-fashioned. In Latin, *stratum* meant *a thing spread*, as a blanket or floor-covering is spread. In England, the word seems to have first come into everyday use during the 1680s, notably with the naturalist John Ray (Derham, 1718). From then until the middle part of the 18th century a collective term, the *Strata*, was commonly employed to indicate a specific group of major rock-layers or 'formations' which from the top downward, as Strachey named them, were: Chalk, Freestone, Lias, Marl, Red Earth, and Coal. As a body, the *Strata* stretched across England from the southwest coast to the northeast coast, and generally pitched or inclined to the east or southeast, so that their bassets or outcropping edges tended to face westward.

Smith's contemporaries dropped the use of *stratum* in favour of *stratified deposit*, by which they intended to explain that these rocks were made of deposited matter, accumulations of particles, that through the passage of time had compacted together; and by repetitions of the process had piled up successive layers, one upon another. The understanding of strata first adopted by Smith was, like Strachey's own, that they had originated by unique fiat in a single act of simultaneous creation at the beginning of the world. That Biblical fact, taught in all the school-rooms of England, offered no reason to suppose that the strata might conceal among themselves significant differences of age. In fact, Smith's magnificent map of 1815 – *A Delineation of the Strata of England and Wales, with part of Scotland* - still demonstrates stratigraphical mapping of immaculate quality, achieved without reference either to relative ages among strata or the nature of geological time.

William Smith's Geology After 1801

Smith's stratigraphical enterprise after 1801 grew into a work-programme of exact mapping through the whole of England, over some 50,000 square miles of territory, lasting 11 years. All this effort was unsupported, costly, and exhausting labour, funded at his own expense, and carried out in addition to other more pressing commissions needed to provide vital subsistence for himself, and later for his wife also. In 1802, Smith formed a land-surveying partnership with Jeremiah Cruse, and opened an office in Bath at the corner of Trim Street (Figure 11).

Ten years of arduous consultancy, from 1802 to 1811, presented Smith with a multitude of opportunities to observe and note the landscapes and geological features of England

Figure 11, The former Smith and Cruse premises at the comer of Trim Street, off Barton Street and near the County Court in central Bath; still in trade as Trim Bridge Galleries.

and Wales. During those years, he was engaged in at least ten coal borings and colliery surveys. Among other projects, there were several large marine-defence works and water management tasks inland. At this time he began to describe himself as a civil engineer. Though Smith's fame now rests on his achievements in geology, particularly on his great map of 1815, he was equally famed during his lifetime as a highly skilled surveyor and civil engineer, especially in matters of water-control and coal prospecting.

Some time previously, in 1804, Smith leased a house in London, where he set up his fossil collection for viewing. It was ingeniously arranged, each stratum represented by a sloping shelf, as if emerging from the ground in a stratigraphic sequence; and each shelf displaying its appropriate suite of fossils. This kind of demonstration illustrated the physical basis for Smith's *Stratigraphical System of Organized Fossils*, which he brought out in 1817. It was a new and radical way to present stratigraphy, but was evidently too radical for some of the capital's connoisseurs of geology who visited Smith's display. Their unimaginative response offered only paltriness and condescension for his pains. Shortly afterwards, a group of them set out on the road to barefaced piracy, publishing a map under the name of the President of the Geological Society that was virtually indistinguishable from Smith's own work. Their action forced Smith out of the market and drove him toward bankruptcy. Leading figures among scientists of the time belittled his work, even though his observations and deductions were self-evidently true. Nevertheless, two of the Geological Society's most able members, William Fitton and Adam Sedgwick gave Smith their decisive and eloquent support, silencing the scoffers. Sedgwick then in 1831 pressed beyond ordinary praise, launching Smith into the role of patriarch, publicly declaring him *Father of English Geology*. Thereafter, the practical usefulness of Smith's ideas to agriculture, engineering, and science came to be widely admitted; and by mid-century a rising popular belief in the utility of science was being celebrated in two huge exhibitions mounted in 1851 and 1862.

In this new mid-century environment of utilitarian virtue, Smith could be presented as a man distinguished in British scientific endeavour, and was suitably shown in a group portrait at the Royal Institution, standing between Sir Joseph Banks and Henry Cavendish. Other admirers of Smith, mostly geologists, began to envelop him in a transfiguring cloud of scholarly reverence, giving him central place in a very British story of a young orphan-boy from nowhere, who defeated adversity through self-help, who succeeded magnificently, unaided and alone in a huge personal enterprise, who confounded his critics, and was during his lifetime proved to have made a great scientific discovery, yet was in the end openly cheated by a parcel of scheming gentry.

ITINERARY OF SITES IN BATH CITY

Bath is not an easy place in which to use a car, though not impossible. There is a helpful Park-and-Ride service in operation. Sites of scientific interest in the city are detailed in a leaflet entitled *Bath Scientific Heritage Trail*, issued originally by the West of England Branch of the British Association, but obtainable together with other information from the *Bath Tourism and Conference Bureau, Abbey Chambers, Abbey Churchyard, Bath BA1 1LY.* One might also view the Bath tourism web site at *www. visitbath.co.uk.*

No.29 Great Pulteney Street

The whole length of this street is part of the Bathwick development scheme commenced in 1788 by the architect Thomas Baldwin. The house numbered 29 became the Bath residence of one of Smith's supporters, the Revd Joseph Townsend (1739-1816), Rector of Pewsey, Wiltshire. He was a considerable author in medicine and cosmogony, 'standing six foot six in his socks, with a voice to match'. His *Character of Moses Established*, which came out in 1813, is expensively sought today for its early printed version of Smith's stratigraphy. A bronze plaque was attached to the house in 1926, inscribed with these words:

Figure 12. Bronze plaque affixed to the wall of No.29 Great Pulteney Street, the Bath residence in 1799 of Joseph Townsend. Photograph courtesy J. T. Greensmith.

Strata.
1. Chalk . . . .
2. Sand . . . .
3. Clay. . . . .
4. Sand and Stone
5. Clay. . . . .
6. Forest Marble
7. Freestone . . . .
8. Blue Clay . . . .
9. Yellow Clay . .
10. Fuller's Earth
11. Bastard ditto, and Sundries
12. Freestone . . . .
13. Sand . . . .
14. Marl Blue . . . .
15. Lias Blue . . . .
16. Ditto White . .
17. Marl Stone, Indigo and Black Marl . . . .
18. Red-ground . .
19. Millstone.
20. Pennant Street
21. Grays . . . .
22. Cliff. . . . .
23. Coal. . . . .

'In this house William Smith the Father of English geology dictated the Order of the Strata December 11, 1799'

The date on the plaque should be June 11, 1799, not December (Figure 12). According to Benjamin Richardson (1758-1832), Smith was in Bath for the annual meeting in June, 1799 of the Bath Agricultural Society. The gathering at Townsend's residence took place only a few weeks after the termination in April 1799 of Smith's employment with the Somersetshire Coal Canal Company.

Richardson had the highest regard for Smith's abilities, and was first among his mentors and advocates. It was Richardson who wrote out the *Order of the Strata* from Smith's dictation, and it was this manuscript in Richardson's handwriting that Smith donated years later to the Geological Society of London. Figure 13, from John Phillips's *Memoirs of William Smith* (1844) lists the twenty-three named strata. According to Richardson's recollection, after writing out the *Order of the Strata*, additional copies of it were given away 'in consequence of Mr. Smith's desire to make so valuable a discovery universally known', which discovery was of the special relationship existing between particular strata and the fossils contained within them. Smith had already demonstrated the truth of this to Richardson and Townsend in the country south and west of Bath, notably at Dundry Hill; and his perception of a predictable sequence of identifiable strata made possible a new and more scientific approach to mineral prospecting in stratified rocks, primarily in pursuit of coal to stoke the furnaces of industry and millions of urban grates. Sinking and boring for coal at Batheaston provides an early example (see below).

Figure 13. (left) William Smith's list of the strata, 1799, copied from the original dictated to Benjamin Richardson at 29, Great Pulteney Street, Bath, and published in Memoirs of William Smith by John Phillips (1844, p.30).

23

Figure 14. North aspect of William Smith's residence in Bath from 1795 to 1798, the middle house in a row known to him as Cottage Crescent. Photograph courtesy W. H. George.

Trim Street

This building (Figure 11) constructed in 1799 at the corner of Trim Street and Trim Bridge, though somewhat misidentified in the past by reason of altered house-numbering, was from 1802 to 1805 the office of William Smith and his land-surveying partner Jeremiah Cruse (1758-1819). Here, Smith's fossil collections were laid out stratigraphically in boxes, open to public view. At this time, Bath's extraordinary social standing and popularity, its innumerable visitors from all walks of life – land owners, urban gentry, collectors of 'cabinet curiosities' – meant this was one of the most effective ways by which Smith's practical results in the field of soil identity and agricultural improvement could be publicly advertised. Smith was at heart a man for whom a working demonstration was more effective than a printed publication.

Bloomfield Crescent

In the autumn of 1795, Smith moved from his lodgings at Rugbourne Farm on the Jones estate, to the middle house (Figure 14) with weather-vane, in this crescent of seven overlooking Bath from the road up to Odd Down (ST 738629). The entrance from Bloomfield Road opens to the rear of the Crescent, and residents may seek a plausible explanation from visitors asking to see the front of the Crescent.

Construction of these houses, then called Cottage Crescent, began in 1794. Smith was here until 1798, supervising work on the Somersetshire Coal Canal. From the front of the Crescent looking northward residents enjoy spectacular views over Bath and the Avon valley. 'From this point,' wrote Smith, 'the eye roved anxiously over the interesting expanse which extended before me ….. then did a thousand thoughts occur to me respecting the geology of that and adjacent districts continually under my eye.' He was already aware from excavation of the canal-bed that fossil occurrence varied from stratum to stratum, and that particular fossils could be associated with particular strata, though he had not yet embarked on any stratigraphic mapping beyond the area of a local publication entitled *Map of 5 miles round the City of Bath*. Smith ended his residence at the Crescent in 1798, when he purchased the house called Tucker Mill or Tucking Mill, near Midford, closer to his Coal Canal work.

Batheaston Coal Trial, 1804-1813

William Smith's involvement in coal-exploration at Batheaston dates from 1804, while he was advising on remedial work for the City's hot springs. The boring for coal at Batheaston was one of the first mineral prospects in Britain to be stratigraphically monitored, and has its own memorial in the name *Coalpit Road*; which branches off London Road at ST 78056743. The actual site of the borehole 'believed to be substantially correct'

is at ST 78186774 (Kellaway, 1991, p.27), on the present-day Elmhurst housing estate.

Between 1791 and 1799 Smith had worked out the sequence of strata around Bath, enabling him, after leaving the Somersetshire Coal Canal Company, to apply his skill to sub-surface exploration for coal, a stratum which he knew to occupy a determinate position in the sequence. Knowing also of the strongly discordant relationship in this part of the country between the *Red-ground* (Triassic) and underlying coal-bearing strata, as illustrated by his copy of John Strachey's cross-section, and the actualities of coal-working at Newton St Loe, barely three miles from Bath city-centre, he could predict that coal might be found by sinking through Lias and Red-ground. This was the case at Batheaston, where his advice was sought, though one must add that the choice of location for the trial had not been his.

Two masonry-lined shafts, each nine-feet in diameter were started, and encountered copious water flows from the Lias. This water was walled off, and in 1808 Smith made a log of the strata penetrated down to that level (Kellaway,1991 p.51-53); but in 1811, after the bottom- hole boring had entered Dolomitic Conglomerate or '*Millstone*' (Triassic) a huge influx of water overwhelmed the pumps. Curiously, this water felt distinctly tepid, some thirteen degrees Fahrenheit above the ambient norm, and rumours flew about that Bath's main asset, the hot springs, were being compromised.

Smith was thus presented with a classic conflict of interest. He knew as a fact by 1811 that the rate of flow at the hot-springs had been altered by the cataract at Batheaston, yet he was expected still to advise on the coal trial. Larger pumps could hardly cope with the water, and boring continued with great difficulty and expense, ending at a total depth of 671 feet, when the Company's money ran out. The trial was abandoned in 1813.

Flowing water can still be seen emerging from an outfall at ST 77956775 on the west side of Coalpit Road, 260 yards ESE of the church of St John the Baptist (ST 77756790).

The barren strata immediately below the Triassic seem to have been sandstones formerly called Millstone Grit, in the uppermost part of the local Carboniferous Limestone sequence, and thus stratigraphically below any productive coal seams. The failure of this attempt to find coal at Batheaston was, of course, unpredictable, and only hindsight could allow the claim that it had been tried for the right geological reasons, and 'only just failed' (Torrens, 2001, p.69). More pertinently, one can be certain that the site was not chosen by William Smith, but by Thomas Walters, owner both of the land and the mineral rights where the operations took place.

Using similar knowledge of stratigraphic sequence, Smith was able to advise also at places where any success in coal-exploration would be virtually impossible. Such an opportunity first came about in 1805 at South Brewham, a Somerset village 18 miles south of Bath. On the evidence of fossil *Gryphaea* from a shaft already sunk to 120 feet depth in search of coal, Smith advised the operators that they were far too high in the stratigraphic sequence ever to reach their objective by boring, and that they had been misled from the beginning by the dark and 'coaly' appearance of local *clunch* soil (Oxford Clay).

ITINERARY OF SITES SOUTH OF BATH

To travel by a more or less chronological route, leave Bath on A36 West, and turn southwest on A39 for Corston and Marksbury. Fork right at Marksbury on A368 to Chelwood cross- roads (ST 625619) and remain on A368 to Sutton Court. A lane on the right (ST599608) goes to a pair of recently built lodges at the head of an avenue leading to the house.

Sutton Court

'This old house is of no importance in itself, it is no Longleat or Hatfield, yet it touches the main course of English history, from the time of Edward the Confessor to the present day And so long as the old walls remain …. there will be two or three persons in each generation in whom they will awaken and keep alive a sense of the reality of English history which cannot be got by books alone.'
Sir Edward Strachey, Bt., 1895

Approaching Sutton Court (ST 596604) on A368 from Chelwood, arable fields reveal red Triassic soil (Figure 15) which overlie Coal Measures. Signposts to the right indicate ways to Stanton Wick and Stanton Drew, old coal-mining areas; and beyond them are elevated tracts of Lower Jurassic about Dundry Hill, capped by Middle Jurassic (Inferior Oolite) limestone.

Until 1973, Sutton Court (Figure 16) was the residence of Sir Edward Strachey, Second Baron Strachie (1882-1973), last in direct line of descent from John Strachey, F.R.S. The house still appears much as it did in former times, though is now a multiple-apartment condominium. In the view from the main avenue approaching the house from the north the outer wall, the tower and its prominent stair-turret, were part of a 14th-century castle. The buttressed wing to the left (northeast) was an Elizabethan parlour and chapel. Most of the stonework has the colour and appearance of Upper Carboniferous Pennant Sandstone. Much remodelling took place in the mid-nineteenth century by Sir Henry Strachey and his architect Thomas Wyatt.

John Strachey was born here on May 10, 1671. He inherited the estate when aged three, spent a short time at Oxford and the Middle Temple, and later developed wide interests in map-making and antiquities. The Royal Society in 1719 published his first geological paper, and elected him to Fellowship. The paper included a detailed horizontal cross-section of the country around Sutton Court, described below.

John Strachey's Section of the Strata, 1719

Strachey's first stratigraphic cross-section (Figure 3) represents strata both underground and at the surface along a line from the lower slopes of Dundry Hill (at the right-hand end) near Norton Hawkfield (ST 593648), extending in a southeasterly direction by Stowey toward Farrington Gurney (ST 628556). It was the first measured horizontal section to appear in English geological literature. Strachey specified twenty-two subdivisions of strata, the

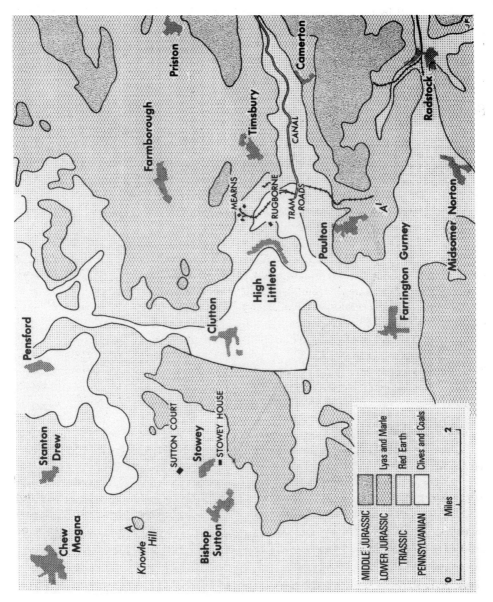

Figure 15. Geological reference map of the area around Sutton Court, Stowey, Farrington Gurney, and High Littleton. Courtesy American Association of Petroleum Geologists (Bulletin, v.53, 1969, p.2261). 'Pennsylvanian' is Upper Carboniferous Coal Measures.

28

Figure 16   The northern aspect of Sutton Court, 1962, still appearing much as it did in John Strachey's time. Sir Edward Strachey (1882-1973) was the last direct descendant to reside here.

thicknesses of all but two of them given, descending from Lower Jurassic at ground surface, through Triassic to a point about 300 feet into the Upper Carboniferous. Such discriminating observation and measurement was altogether new and original. At first sight, the section might seem somewhat crude, but closer inspection reveals that it is certainly not. For example:

(a) Strachey says in his 1719 paper that in the area discussed all the coals 'pitch or rise about twenty-two inches in a fathom,' which is a slope or dip of 17°, Measuring the illustration will reveal that the engraver varied slightly from 17° to 19°. Current Geological Survey maps show a dip of 18°.

(b) Strachey's thickness measurements of the coals and intervening strata found in pits at Bishop Sutton (about a mile southwest from Sutton Court) accord very well with later observations. The collieries to which he referred had disappeared before the 19th century, though records from later pits nearby show that the measurements were accurate, and names that he used for individual strata continued in use until mining ceased.

Professor D. T. Donovan, visiting the area in December 1987, gave further consideration to this cross-section:

'Strachey's section also shows shafts commencing in (Blue) Lias, and therefore penetrating the whole thickness of the Trias; the shaft at the right-hand (NW) end of his section would have had to sink through about 200 feet of Mesozoic before reaching Coal Measures.
Strachey wrote (1719, p.968) that his section was about four miles long and extended from NW to SE. This raises several points. The section is probably idealised, but if it is not wholly imaginary, then the NW end must be at the southern slopes of Dundry Hill, where the place-name Blacklands (ST 582641), on the Blue Lias outcrop, does indeed suggest the presence of old coal tips. The right-hand valley in the section would then be the Chew valley at Stanton Drew, and the left-hand one the Cam valley. The fault ('Ridg') could be the Clutton Fault.
The seams listed by Strachey agree in a general way with the Bromley seams, the Peacock or Peau Vein, with 'cockle-shells and fern branches' in the 'cliff' above it being perhaps Bromley no.4, which has fossil plants and *Anthraconauta* in the shale above it (G.A. Kellaway, pers. comm.). Strachey's Stinking Vein, the highest, would be Bromley no.1 and so on'
See also Kellaway and Welch (1993, p.109-111).

The abandoned site of Bromley Colliery at (ST 607618) by the A368, is one mile northeast of Sutton Court. The mine closed in 1957.
From Sutton Court, return to A368 and turn right, i.e. southward, going a few yards to the Stowey turn-off, where a space by the telephone-box allows a short stop to view the front or south aspect of Sutton Court.

Stowey, and the Jones Inheritance

At the far end of the village (ST 599594), the view looking northward from Castle Hill (Figure 17) was represented by Strachey on the right-hand half of his cross-section (Figure 3). He showed the high ground of *Lyas* and *Marle* (Lower Jurassic) rising above the *Red Earth* (Triassic) where Stowey House and the adjacent church stand (ST 598595). Southeastward, on the other side of Castle Hill, his line of section crossed an area of exposed Coal Measures near Farrington Gurney, where Strachey showed a pit sunk to the *Three Coal Veyn*. Farther to the southeast, at the left-hand termination of his section, Strachey indicated more hills of *Lyas* and *Marle* around Paulton. What strikes a present-day reader about this cross-section, more than anything else, is its air of modernity.' It conveys,' said Sir Edward Bailey,'As clear a picture as could be desired of a semi-concealed coalfield' But therein lurks a hazard, because it is *not* modern. Strachey was illustrating the angular discordance between Coal Measures and overlying Lyas as known to colliers, but not *unconformity*, which in his day described the ecclesiastical attitude of a dissenting cleric.

William Smith enters this story forty-eight years after John Strachey's death, when in 1791 his employer at Stow-on-the-Wold offered him a commission from Lady Elizbeth Jones of Ramsbury to make a probate survey of an estate at Stowey, which she had inherited from John Strachey's niece. In addition to the house and land at Stowey the property included lands and a colliery at High Littleton, and an old manor house called Rugbourne, where Smith found lodging with a tenant farmer.

Rugbourne Farm, High Littleton

From Stowey, join the A37 near Clutton at ST 619589, travelling south to White Cross, where turn east on A39 to High Littleton. There is a small recreation ground with free parking (ST 648582) a few yards down a lane leading to Timsbury, The old manor house of Rugbourne (Figure 18) at ST 652584 is now a working farm where car parking may not be welcomed, but good views can be had from the recreation ground, and across Timsbury bottom to the site of Mearns Colliery on Amesbury Hill.

Rugbourne lies a quarter of a mile east of High Littleton, about halfway between the village and the site of Mearns coal pit. It is of 17th-century construction, three-storeyed with a twin-gabled roof, and moulded plasterwork ceilings. Smith arrived here in October, 1791. 'I resided,' he wrote in his reminiscences, 'in a part of the large old manor house belonging to Lady Jones [of Ramsbury], called Rugburn. Coal was worked at High Littleton beneath the red earth, and I was desired to investigate the collieries'. Smith lodged here from 1791 to 1795 for 'half a guinea a week plus half a crown for his horse.'

A document found among Smith's papers at Oxford, signed and dated 14th July, 1792, reflects his acute awareness that here at High Littleton lay possible future employment. He drew up for himself a paper (Figure 19) headed: *'Proposal of Mr Wm. Smith of Stow, Gloucestershire, to Lady Jones as to being admitted a Partner in her Coal Works at High Littleton'*. A note added says that it was copied at Ramsbury Manor on January 2nd, 1793. Unfortunately, Lady Elizabeth Jones of Ramsbury died soon afterwards, and nothing came of Smith's proposal; but in view of his subsequent career with the Somersetshire Coal Canal proprietors, this document suggests that he was already canvassing for a more permanent

Figure 17. At Stowey, a view northward from the hill of Lias at the middle of Strachey's cross-section,1719. Beyond Stowey House, Sutton Court is just visible among trees, and in the distance is Dundry Hill. A memorial in the church records the death in 1791 of Strachey's niece, Mary Jones.

Figure 18. Rugbourne House, southeast aspect. William Smith had lodgings here between 1791 and 1795 while making a probate survey of the estate for Lady Elizabeth Jones. He recalled late in life that 'there was a square, walled court in front, with entrance gates.'

employment in the neighbourhood of High Littleton, rather than returning to Stow-on-the-Wold.

Mearns Colliery

In 1783, eight partners obtained leases and authority to get coal here. The initial shaft for the colliery was sunk between Limekiln Ground and Great Mearns near ST 65255880 (Figure 5), on land belonging to John Strachey's niece, Mary Jones. Smith surveyed this coal-work in 1792, and as so often in Smith's career, the only account of events attending his arrival is to be found in John Phillips's *Memoirs of William Smith* (1844, p.6).

Mearns colliery worked coals in the Upper or Radstock Group of the local Coal Measures, not the Lower or Farrington Coals featured in Strachey's sections. At the Mearns colliery coal seams dipped eastward into a structural basin centered some two miles away near Camerton. Before the Coal Canal was built, hewn coal was taken away by pack-animals. Mearns was closed in 1824, and the waste-tips were scarified in the 1950s and early 1960s, leaving almost no visible trace.

Proposal of Mr Wm Smith of Stow Gloucestershire to Lady Jones as to being admitted a Partner in her Coal works at High Littleton

If admitted a Partner for 1/8th or 1/4 part of either of the two new works now going on (such 1/8th or 1/4 part to be taken out of Lady Jones's present share) — Mr Smith would inspect those Works & accounts as well as the old Works (with respect to the common Course of that business) for 20 £ per annum; but when new Levels were drove or great alterations made that required to be measured and mapped to be paid for such extra business —

If Lady Jones should open a new Pit on exclusive Work independent of the present Partners & would admit Mr Smith to 1/8th or 1/4th (instead of the above Works) he would inspect such new Work and also those above mentioned for the same Salary with an addition of another 20 £ per annum in Case he takes upon himself the payment of the Men, or, in other Words, assumes the same Office at this Pitt that Bush has at the present Works, which consists in paying the Men & settling the Accounts —

Mr Smith to be at every expence in the working the share allotted him, whether an Eight or fourth — and to make regular returns to Lady Jones of the State of the Works from time to time —

14th July 1792

Wm Smith

-- Copied at Ramsbury Manor, Jan: 2nd 1793 --

Figure 19. William Smith's proposal of 1792 to Lady Elizabeth Jones of Ramsbury, hoping to find continuing employment on her property.

Figure 20.   Timsbury basin and wharfmaster's cottage, 1962. The magnificent stand of elms succumbed soon after.

The Somersetshire Coal Canal

The site of Timsbury Basin and wharfage at the canal terminus (ST 655577) is about half a mile southeast from the High Littleton recreation ground. From the entrance, turn right, then almost immediately left, and left again into a lane going down to Gossard Bridge and a sewage works, where there is footpath access to the former canal basin. In recent years it has been somewhat reshaped as a 'wildlife reserve,' and little can be seen beyond a depression in the ground where the canal was, and an overgrown colliery-waste tip. Figure 20 illustrates the scene as it was in 1962, while the wharfmaster's house still stood, and grass-covered heaps of debris remained on the wharf. Useful old maps of this and other important sites on the Canal were published by Chapman (1988).

Late in 1792 proposals were made in the district for a canal to serve the mines, and a newly formed Canal Committee, having received favourable reports of William Smith's surveying work on Lady Jones's properties, engaged him in 1793 to take levels along the proposed route of the canal. As originally projected, it was to have a main line going down the valley of the Cam, taking coal from mines around High Littleton and Paulton, and a branch

35

Figure 21. At the top lock of the Combe Hay flight, Somersetshire Coal Canal. This view emphasises the difference of elevation between the Coal Canal's upper level and the floor of the Cam valley below. Behind the tree-trunk at the left, light reflects from the original cut going to the site of the abandoned caisson-lift. Photograph about 1880, courtesy Robin Athill, Downside Abbey.

of the canal carrying coal from Radstock down the valley of Wellow brook to a junction at Midford, from where a single waterway would join the Kennet and Avon Canal near Limpley Stoke. This plan would enable coal traffic to connect easily with the City of Bath, and towns to the east in Wiltshire.

Unfortunately, the Coal Canal would encounter two major ground-elevation difficulties, one at Combe Hay on the main line coming from Timsbury terminus, and another on the southern branch at Twinhoe, about a mile south of Midford. The southern branch never reached completion, and was terminated near Middle Twinhoe (ST 756594) where, among thickets of wild vegetation, the excavated hollow of the terminal basin can still be found. A tram road was made to carry coal from this basin down to a wharf which, by means of a small aqueduct (ST 758605) connected to the main line of the Coal Canal (Figure 10, Inset B). The tram road was later extended back from Twinhoe to Radstock, laid on the levelled grade of the towing path beside the empty canal-bed. Convincing geological evidence exists

36

for this expensive change of plan, the cause being an early and rapid failure of water supply, forcing abandonment of work on a canal link between Radstock and the wharf at Midford (Torrens 1976, p.37).

The main, or northern branch of the coal canal commenced at Timsbury Basin (ST 657577), close to Paulton Engine pit in the Cam valley, about midway between Rugbourne and Paulton village. This colliery, the earliest in the area after Mearns, was at work in 1791. It had an atmospheric or 'fire' engine to lift water from a depth of more than 600 feet. Wharves at Timsbury Basin received coal coming down by tram-road from about eighteen pits, nine from the north (of which Mearns was one) and nine from the south. Tenders for constructing these tram roads were invited in May and July of 1795, and shipments of coal from Timsbury to Dunkerton wharf began in November, 1799.

The second ground-elevation difficulty was at Combe Hay, on the northern main line. The plan called for an upper canal-level between the Timsbury terminus and Combe Hay, and a lower one from Combe Hay via Midford to the junction with the Kennet and Avon Canal. At Combe Hay, the elevation difference between the surveyed upper level and the floor of the Cam valley below was about 130 feet (Figure 21). Ten years of engineering contrivance eventually overcame this problem, beginning with an ambitiously innovative hydrostatic lift, the failure of which in 1799 cost William Smith his employment on the canal. The proprietors then built an inclined plane to connect the two levels, though it was soon abandoned in favour of a tightly-looped flight of twenty-two conventional locks (Inset A of Figure 10, Figure 22, and Figure 23). The system of locks succeeded, and was in use from 1804 to 1899. In its heyday the canal carried 150,000 tons of coal a year, but decline had set in by mid-century. Evidence offered to the 1906 Royal Commission on canals stated among other things that strikes in the Radstock area drove away trade, and opening of the Severn Tunnel brought cheaper Welsh coal into the district; but the fundamental cause of decline was the greater commercial efficiency of carriage by rail, and the aggressive acquisition of canal properties by railway companies. In the case of the Somersetshire Coal Canal, the Royal Commission was told:

'What did more than anything was that about 1870 the Somerset and Dorset Railway purchased the tramway owned by the Somerset Coal Canal, which connected that canal with the Radstock collieries. They purchased it for £20,000 under the powers of an Act of Parliament [August 1871]. That crippled the canal trade by cutting off the collieries from the canal'.

Landowners adjoining the remaining part of the canal in 1902 applied for a warrant of closure and abandonment, on the ground that the canal was 'derelict and dangerous,' again as recorded by the Royal Commission:

The canal 'was never likely to be re-opened, the collieries which it had served having been closed. The Great Western Railway Company offered to purchase the site of the canal, and proposed to apply to Parliament for powers to construct a railway thereon. The canal was abandoned, and the site vested in the Great Western Railway Company, by that Company's Act of 1904.'

Figure 22. Magnified detail from an aerial view showing part of the Combe Hay flight of locks, and the mains of the inclined plane used for trans-shipping coal from the upper to the lower level of the Canal. Inset A of Figure 10 identifies some of the features visible in this 1947 photograph. Low incident sunlight emphasises shadows cast by trees. Locks number 14, 15, and 17, are indicated on the photograph. Lock 16 was destroyed when the railway was built, though Boyling's house, featured in Figure 23, is just visible beside the empty approach pond, about midway between the figures 15 and 17. North is to the left.

Figure 23. A road bridge crossed the entrance to Lock 16 in the flight of twenty-two locks joining the upper and lower levels of the Canal at Combe Hay. The bridge came to an end when the G.W.R. branch line was built, but Boyling's house survived. Photograph dated September,1892, courtesy Mrs Boyling, 1962.

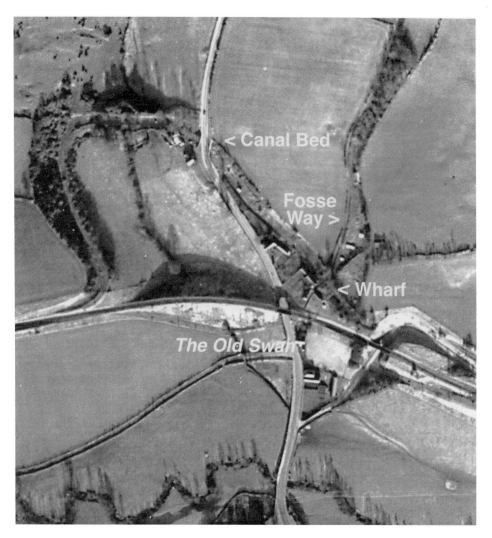

Figure 24. Aerial view of the A367 road by the Old Swan, Dunkerton, in 1947. Remains of the old Coal Canal bed, Dunkerton Wharf, and the G.W.R. branch line passing behind the Old Swan are clearly visible. North is to the top.

The line built by the G.W.R. was a single-track laid partly over the course of the old canal. It faced the same elevation difference at Combe Hay which had been so difficult for the canal builders. The railway Company's solution was a three-mile ramp from Midford to Combe Hay carrying the track to the upper level. The chief purpose of this railway was to

40

serve new mines opened in 1906 at Camerton and Dunkerton, but failure at Dunkerton in 1927, falling production and eventual closure of Camerton in 1950, left this G. W .R. branch line with no purpose, its short life at an end, *in memoriam carbonarium* 1907-1951.

Dunkerton Wharf and the Fosse Way

From High Littleton, the B3115 provides a convenient route by way of former coal-mining settlements at Tyning, Timsbury and Tunley, to the junction with A367 (ST 719608). Turn south, and on the west side of A367, stop at a telephone box and lay-by (ST 716597).

On the opposite side of the road, a track leads along the towing path of the Coal Canal, its bed filled with rubbish and weedily overgrown. The Parliamentary six-milestone, minus plate, stands on the canal bank. These stones were set up at half-mile intervals, measuring the distance from the junction of the Somersetshire Coal Canal with the Kennet and Avon Canal at Dundas Aqueduct. Figure 24, an aerial photograph, shows the main features of the area - the loop of the Canal round the hillside, remains of a single-span aqueduct at the head of this loop, the Fosse Way, the site of Dunkerton Wharf, and the Old Swan.

From the main road, follow the towpath southeastward for 150 yards to the intersection with an old bridle road, now a public footpath. This is the site of a former bridge over the canal (Figure 25). On each side of it were coal wharves. This was the eastern terminus of the first section of the canal to be brought into operation, when in October 1798 coals from Camerton were unloaded and taken by pack-animals down to Bath.

The old bridle road going uphill from Dunkerton Wharf is the Fosse Way, an immensely long Roman alignment, more than 400 miles, connecting Axminster in Devon with Lincoln and country beyond. The Fosse Way was not one of the many roads radiating from London, but a cross-country means of military communication that would have been wanted at an early stage in the Claudian conquest of AD 47, consolidating the frontier between what was securely Roman and what was not.

Proceed on foot southwards, downhill about 200 yards to the Old Swan (ST 716596).

Dunkerton, the Old Swan Inn

This house (Figure 26), now tastelessly disfigured, was once an inn serving travellers on the Fosse Way. It is the actual place where William Smith, on January 5, 1796, wrote his famous ten-line memorandum affirming that Nature had arranged fossils in a regular order, and had assigned to each class its own stratum.

By following the progress of construction on the Coal Canal it is possible to give a particular reason for this date in January 1796, and this place. Tenders for excavating the canal bed were called in two-mile sections starting in June 1795 from Paulton Engine colliery on the northern branch, and from Radstock on the southern branch. Both of these sections were on Triassic bedrock (the unfossiliferous Triassic *Red-ground*). The next section on the main line, for which a contractor was engaged in September, 1795, extended to the Dunkerton *Swan*, and was cut mainly in Lower and Middle Jurassic strata (Lower Lias, Midford Sand, and Inferior Oolite). By the end of 1795, William Smith, who then was officially 'the

Figure 25. Dunkerton Wharf on the Somersetshire Coal Canal as it was in 1890. This wharf opened to coal-traffic in 1799, and by 1899 it was virtually derelict. A stone bridge (now vanished) carried the Fosse Way over the Canal. Nevertheless, at least two buildings to the left of the picture remain standing and are recognisable. Photograph courtesy Bath and Wilts Evening Chronicle.

Surveyor' would have been aware from his instrumental levelling that Triassic and Jurassic strata exposed by the excavations were dipping gently in an easterly direction, each one in turn dropping below the plane of his surveyed level. By January 1796, excavation of the northern cut as far as Dunkerton had progressively exposed rocks up to *Freestone* (No.12 in Smith's 1799 standard sequence, Figure 13); while the southern cut was in *Red-ground* (No. 18 of his 1799 standard). Smith could see from these results of surveyed levelling on the two branches of the canal that the *Red-ground* and overlying strata were not in fact quite horizontal as Strachey's colliers had reported, but were dipping toward the southeast. 'On this matter,' he said, 'I began to think for myself'.

Figure 26. The Old Swan, Dunkerton, 1962. Here on January 5th, 1796, William Smith wrote his famous memorandum on fossils stating that to each class was assigned its peculiar stratum. Remains of the Coal Canal, which Smith was at that time surveying, can be found 100 yards up the hill behind the house.

Combe Bay, Rowley Farm and Caisson House

Because of narrow passing places, two sites, one at Combe Hay and the other at Tucking Mill can not be conveniently approached by vehicles larger than a minibus. Turn east from A367 into the lane by the garden wall of the Old Swan, and proceed eastward toward Combe Hay, watching for sign-posts at awkward turns. About a quarter of a mile east of Combe Hay village a fork to the left leads to Rowley Farm and Caisson House (ST 740602).

This is private property, though also an area of significant industrial heritage where a 'patent hydrostatic or caisson lock' engineered by Robert Weldon was built and tested between 1796 and 1797. Its site here is shown by Inset A of Figure 10. The device was conceived as a novel and efficient method of moving boats vertically, while afloat and loaded, between upper and lower levels of a waterway, doing so by means of a closable chamber or caisson moving vertically inside a water-filled shaft. When tested at Combe Hay in June 1798 the device functioned with elegant success, and another was planned lower down as part of a system to overcome the whole elevation difference between the two levels of the Coal Canal. But to everyone's dismay, serious malfunctions soon began to occur, and several

Figure 27. Tucking Mill, near Midford, 2001.

committee people were said later to have been rescued in a state of near suffocation from a jammed caisson. Alarming reports appeared in the *Bath Chronicle*, and in the Company's *Minute Book*. Finally, on December 5th, 1798: 'In consequence of repeated failures of the caisson ...Mr Smith had agreed to take the inspection of the Dunkerton line, &c'. This entry with its unexplained terminal '&c.' seems to have been an elliptical way of saying that William Smith, the Company's Surveyor, was the one to be blamed for these failures. On March 21st, 1799, the *Bath Chronicle* advertised a meeting of proprietors 'to determine finally whether to adopt caissons' and only fifteen days afterwards the *Minute Book* recorded that 'Smith ceases to be surveyor to the company.'

44

In fact, no negligence should have been attributed to Smith; for the problem was geological, not mechanical, being caused by swelling bentonitic clay in the Lower Fullers Earth, which cracked and dislodged masonry blocks lining the shaft, so causing physical obstruction to the caisson's passage within the shaft, and concomitant loss of water. Smith, as the Company's appointed Surveyor of works, would have been deemed responsible for the failure of the caisson-shaft, though its root cause was hardly foreseeable Nevertheless, at the age of thirty Smith found himself no longer employed by the Canal Company.

Tucking Mill, Midford

From the approach road leading to Rowley Farm and Caisson House return to the lane going toward Midford, and descend downhill past relics of Canal Company and G.W.R. operations, including the surviving house by the entrance to the now-obliterated Lock 16 (Figure 23). Continue eastward, crossing B3110 and proceed forward to Tucking Mill. A sham gothic 'castle' on the hill to the left was the home of Charles Connolly, a local landowner who contributed to Smith's financial ruin by foreclosing his mortgage. 'Attended' parking is possible, though not encouraged, at the entrance to the Wessex Water Authority's plant by Tucking Mill (ST 766615).

Richard Warner's *Excursions from Bath* in 1801 brought this house (Figure 27) into public notice, extolling its owner's geological knowledge and hinting of a forthcoming publication that would present a new 'system of geology.' More than likely, Warner had the *Order of Strata* in mind, the introduction to which Smith had composed by 1801 (Cox, 1942).

'Tucker Mill, a cottage crouching under the high bank that rises above it, and seen from the Midford road, the residence of Mr. Smith, a man whose invincible industry and indefatigable perseverance, unaided by the advantages of fortune or situation, have furnished him with a degree of geological and mineralogical knowledge which few, if any, of his contemporaries possess. Patient observation and practical experience, blended with great natural sagacity, have enabled him to form a system of geology equally new and satisfactory, which, you will hear with pleasure, is intended for the world, when properly digested and arranged'.

The Somersetshire Coal Canal here ran adjacent to the roadway (Figure 28) but has almost disappeared after being used as a Corporation tip. Even in 1962 there were remains of a grass-covered wharf, and a statutory milestone, complete with its one-and-a-half-mile iron plate. Visitors who came on geological field excursions to see William Smith's cottage at Tucking Mill went to the 'wrong' house, to the west of the gateway entrance, with its mistakenly placed memorial stone. Joan Eyles explained in 1974, to anyone who would listen, that:

'The property called Tucking Mill, in the parish of Monkton Combe near Bath,

45

Figure 28. A view of the Coal Canal at Tucking Mill from William Smith's house, in 1889 or soon after. A short distance beyond the bend at Midford village stood an ingenious machine for weighing boat-loads of coals. 'Tolls were paid there,' but by 1899 traffic had practically ceased, 'and when the horse died, the old man and his daughter pulled the boats theirselves.' Photograph from L.R. Cox, 1941.

purchased by William Smith in 1798, still exists, but bears no mark of identification. The nearby Tucking Mill Cottage, in the parish of South Stoke, which bears the tablet *Here lived William Smith* ...is now known to have been wrongly identified as his home'.

Suspicions existed long before Joan Eyles went into print that all was not right, for the Cottage presents a gothic style of fenestration and a wrought-iron porch that was more typical of the 1830s than any time before 1798. The crucial facts exposed by Joan Eyles were discovered in the property deeds of Smith's actual purchase, revealing that the wrongly chosen and memorialised Tucking Mill Cottage was in another parish. Many earnest words have accumulated over the subject of moving the memorial stone to a 'correct' location, but this muddle, now lacking enough obscurity to be forgotten, has become its own memorial.

The house that Smith called home was a narrow ashlar-faced structure, which some time later was doubled in size, more or less, and re-roofed. According to one opinion (Eyles,

1974) the western side of the building as it now stands (to the left, as viewed from the road, (Figure 27) was Smith's original house. To the right, the structure appears to be made from reclaimed material, mason-marked and less well dressed. Note, for instance, the string-course inserted at the second-floor window-level on the east side, bringing that work into line with the opposite work; and note also the late insertion of a third window at ground level on the west side, which was not part of the original. A second view, based on a 'master builder's letter' quoted by R.H.S.Robertson (1986, p.195) and vigorously upheld by H.S. Torrens (2001 p.xxxvi) claims the right-hand side to have been Smith's original, 'built by Smith between 1798 and1801'. Nonetheless, critical visual inspection leaves some doubt, one way or the other. An informed study of this building's structural evolution by an appropriately qualified domestic architect could offer a more secure diagnosis. Even so, the matter is not without its humour, that more than two centuries after Smith purchased his property at Tucking Mill, not every observer is certain what actually it was that he bought. Speculatively, it is not unreasonable to expect that worthwhile information might be obtained from the re-used mason-marked stones, perhaps the demolished upper courses of the abandoned caisson shaft at Combe Hay.

Smith lost possession of this house when his stone-quarrying operations on Combe Down failed, and a claim for unpaid debt was made against him by the gambling Charles Conolly of Midford Castle.

Hill Farm, near Pipehouse, Midford

Return from Tucking Mill to rejoin B3110, and go south through Midford, ascending to the other side of the valley. It is not impossible to park a car for a few minutes by the Hill Farm and Pipehouse entrance (ST 769596) at a sharp bend of the B3110, high on Midford Hill, about 3/4 mile from the village (Hog Wood in Figure 29). Here, near Pipehouse, Smith demonstrated his method of relating a detached outlier or 'insular knoll' to the main body of the parent stratum. In this example, dating from about 1805, he discussed the Cornbrash, which was an additional stratum lying between units 3 and 4 of his 1799 'standard' table of strata in the vicinity of Bath. (Figure 13) At this place Smith identified and described:

'A detached piece of the Cornbrash Stratum (not ten acres) near Pipehouse, south of Bath. It is in the angle of the pasture Field which goes down to Pipehouse It produces a small piece of good land which is common to the soils of the same Stratum about Wolverton [ST 792540] and other places. It was by the extraordinary appearance of this Pasture on the 1st March that I was induced to look for these Fossils well knowing tha no Stratum but the Cornbrash cold produce such Herbage in a situation where Dung is seldom or ever used. The badness of the Land upon the Clay Stratum which is next down the slope gave strength to the Conjecture and the Inspection of the Stone thrown out of the Farm ditch furnished the most indubitable proofs [i.e. fossils] of what I had expected to find.'

Later (1819), Smith added:

Figure 29. Geological map showing the Cornbrash outlier ('g9') at Pipehouse, near Midford. Based on sheet 19 by permission of the British Geological Survey, IPR/52-53C NERC. All rights reserved.

'The Cornbrash, though altogether but a thin rock, has not its organized fossils equally diffused, or promiscuously distributed. The upper beds of stone which compose the rock, contain fossils materially different from those in the under.'

This remarkable observation was overlooked for more than a century, while authors preferred to speak of the Cornbrash as if it were a single homogeneous stratum, indivisible, and remarkable only for its wide distribution and lithic uniformity. In reality the Cornbrash

48

consists of two essentially distinct parts, an Upper and a Lower, which differ widely in their lithology as well as in their fauna (Arkell, 1933, p.326).

Detection of two suites of fossils within the 10-20 feet thickness of Cornbrash, particularly after having determined at Pipehouse that here beneath the vegetation was a detached remnant of it, is one of Smith's most discerning observations. The two suites now form the basis for a Stage boundary in the Jurassic, and the tiny outlier duly appears on Geological Survey maps.

Broadfield Farm, Hinton Charterhouse

Broadfield Farm (ST 767588), on the west side of B3110 is less than half a mile south of the Pipehouse site, and about half a mile north of Hinton Charterhouse village. There is nothing special to see, though this was the home of William Smith's brother John from about 1804 to 1819. He also was a land surveyor and drainer, and assisted William in local professional engagements. Many of Smith's letters surviving from this period were written from Broadfield Farm, where he could shelter from the financial problems arising from his stone-quarrying operations close by his usual residence at Tucking Mill.

Farleigh Hungerford, the Church and Rectory

From Broadfield Farm continue south on B3110 to Norton St Philip, and there turn left on to A366, which goes about two miles directly to Farleigh Hungerford. In addition to links connecting this place with William Smith and his nephew, John Phillips, Farleigh has also the picturesque ruins of a mediaeval castle, built on ransom proceeds for the Duke of Orleans, captured at Agincourt. One can park a car, possibly two, at the gateway to the churchyard, and with permission from the Churchwardens, the key to this usually-locked church can be obtained from the English Heritage Curator of Farleigh Castle, a few yards down the main road at ST 802576.

Smith's good friend and early mentor Benjamin Richardson (1758-1832) was Rector of Farleigh where, in the parish church of St Leonard (ST 800574), there are two memorial tablets honouring him (Figure 30). Some thirty years after Richardson and Joseph Townsend had been astonished by Smith's ability to forecast the fosssils that they would find on Dundry Hill, Adam Sedgwick asked Richardson to describe his memory of that experience. Below is part of Richardson's letter replying to Sedgwick, who was then President of the Geological Society. It was written just before the Society made Smith the first recipient of its highest award, the Wollaston Medal:

'Farley Rectory 10th Feb. 1831
I am requested to present you the particulars of my acquaintance with Mr. William Smith, well known by the appropriate appellation of "Strata Smith". At the annual meeting of the Bath Agricultural Society in 1799, Mr. Smith was introduced to my residence in Bath, when, on viewing my collection of fossils, he told me the beds to which they exclusively belonged, and pointed out some peculiar to each. This, by

Figure 30. Memorial tablet to Benjamin Richardson in the Parish Church of St Leonard, Farleigh Hungerford.

attending him in the fields, I soon found to be the fact, and also that they had a general inclination to the south-east, following each other in regular succession. He wished me to communicate this to the Rev. J. Townsend of Pewsey (then in Bath) we were soon much more astonished by proofs that whatever stratum was found in any part of England, the same remains would be found in it and no other.
I am. Sir, &c., B. Richardson'

The Rectory (Figure 31) from which this letter was sent is next to the church, though is now an ordinary private residence. John Phillips (1800-1874) Smith's nephew and biographer, was here as a schoolboy. Like Smith he had been orphaned in childhood, and partly through the good offices of Richardson attended school at Holt, about four miles from Farleigh. He spent a year here, from 1814 to 1815, with the Richardson family.

Figure 31. The old Rectory, Farleigh Hungerford.

CONCLUDING REMARKS

Stratigraphy, and the geology of strata, originated from the accumulated lore of industrial workmen, chiefly coal miners. Two principal agents who brought about the first considerable growth in knowledge of the strata of England, and its subsequent introduction to science, were John Strachey (1671-1743) and William Smith (1769-1839). The American Association of Petroleum Geologists in 1969 marked the 250th anniversary of Strachey's Description of the Strata, and the 200th anniversary of Smith's birth, with a publication illustrating the historical relationship between industry and stratigraphy, and describing some still unexplained parallels and coincidences found in their published works. Since 1969, though more evidence has come to light of John Strachey's posthumous influence on William Smith's understanding of the strata, a more radical examination of their relationship remains to be made.

This Guide draws much from field-itineraries and excursions organised by the author and Dr Hugh Torrens, modelled with gratitude on parts of the first and much longer visit organised in 1940 by the Geologists' Association (Cox, L.R. *et al.* 1941).

SOURCES AND TEXT REFERENCES

For general reading about the nature of stratigraphy and its place in the history of geology three books can be particularly recommended, viz:
I) D. T. DONOVAN. 1966. *Stratigraphy, an Introduction to Principles*. London, Thomas Murby, pp. 199.
(2) ROY PORTER. 1977. *The Making of Geology, Earth Science in Britain 1660-1815*. Cambridge, pp.288.
(3) JOHN CHALLINOR. 1971. *The History of British Geology, a Bibliographical Study*. London, Barnes & Noble, pp.224.

Another work of particular value, illuminating the life and geological intuitions of William Smith, is a newly-issued reprinting of John Phillips's Memoirs of William Smith, LL.D,.(1844), with an introduction and further complementary text on Smith's industrial activities contributed by Professor H.S. Torrens. It offers more than one might expect from a single volume on the life and times of William Smith, and was published in June, 2003, by the Bath Royal Literary and Scientific Institution (ISBN O 9544 9410 5).

Other citations and sources quoted in the text of this Guide are listed below. This is only a partial and narrowly selective bibliography from a very large literature.

ARKELL, W .J .1933. *The Jurassic System in Great Britain*. Oxford, Clarendon Press, 681 pp.
CHAPMAN, M. 1988. The Somerset Coal Canal, a cartographical survey. Bristol *Industrial Archaeological Society Journal*, 20, 4-22.
COX, L.R. 1941. Easter field meeting, 1940. *Proceedings of the Geologists' Association*, 52, 16-35.
COX, L.R. 1942. New light on William Smith and his work. *Proceedings of the Yorkshire Geological Society*, 25, 1-99.
DEREHAM, W (ed.) 1718. *Philosophical letters between the late learned Mr. Ray and several of his ingenious correspondents*. London, J. Innys, 376 pp.
EYLES, J.M. 1974. William Smith's home near Bath: the real Tucking Mill. *Journal of the Society for the Bibliography of Natural History*, **7**, 29-34.
HARLEY, J.B. 1966. John Strachey of Somerset: an antiquarian cartographer of the early eighteenth century. *Cartographic Journal*, **3**, 2-7.
KELLAWAY, G .A. 1991. The work of William Smith at Bath (1799-1813). In *Hot Springs of Bath*, pp 25-56. Edited by G.A. Kellaway. Bath, City Council.
KELLAWAY, G .A. and WELCH, F .B.A. 1993. *Geology of the Bristol District*. London, H.M.S.O., pp.199.
McGARVIE, M. 1983. John Strachey, F.R.S. and the antiquities of Wessex in 1730. *Ancient Monuments Society's Transactions*, **27**, 77-104.
PHILLIPS, J. 1844. *Memoirs of William Smith, LL.D.*, London, John Murray, pp150. Reprinted New York, Arno. 1978; and Bath, The Bath Royal Literary and Scientific Institution, 2003.

ROBERTSON, R.H.S. 1986. *Fuller 's earth: a history of calcium montmorillonite.* Hythe, Kent, Volturna Press, pp. 421

ROYAL COMMISSION ON CANALS AND WATERWAYS. 1906-1910. Reports, 12 vols London, H.M. Stationery Office.

SMITH WILLIAM. 1819 *Stratigraphical system of organized fossils.* London, E. Williams pp.118. (Pt 4, Cornbrash)

STRACHEY, JOHN. 1719. A curious description of the strata observ'd in the coal-mines of Mendip in Somerset-shire. *Philosophical Transactions of the Royal Society* **30**, 968-973.

STRACHEY, JOHN. 1727. *Observations on the different strata of earths, and minerals.* London, J. Walthoe, pp.16.

TORRENS, H. S. 1976. The Radstock arm of the Somerset Coal Canal. *Bristol Industrial Archaeological Society Journal* **9**, 37.

TORRENS, H. S. 2001. Timeless order: William Smith (1769-1839) and the search for raw materials 1800-1820. In *The age of the Earth from 4004 BC to AD 2002.* Special Publication 190, Geological Society of London, pp.288.